UNDECIPHERABLE *melody*

RASHIDA

Writer's Pocket

First published by Writer's Pocket in 2024

email:publish@writerspocket.com

Copyright © 2024 Rashida M. C.

cover design by Khushi Desai

ISBN-13: 978-93-6083-425-8

www.writerspocket.com

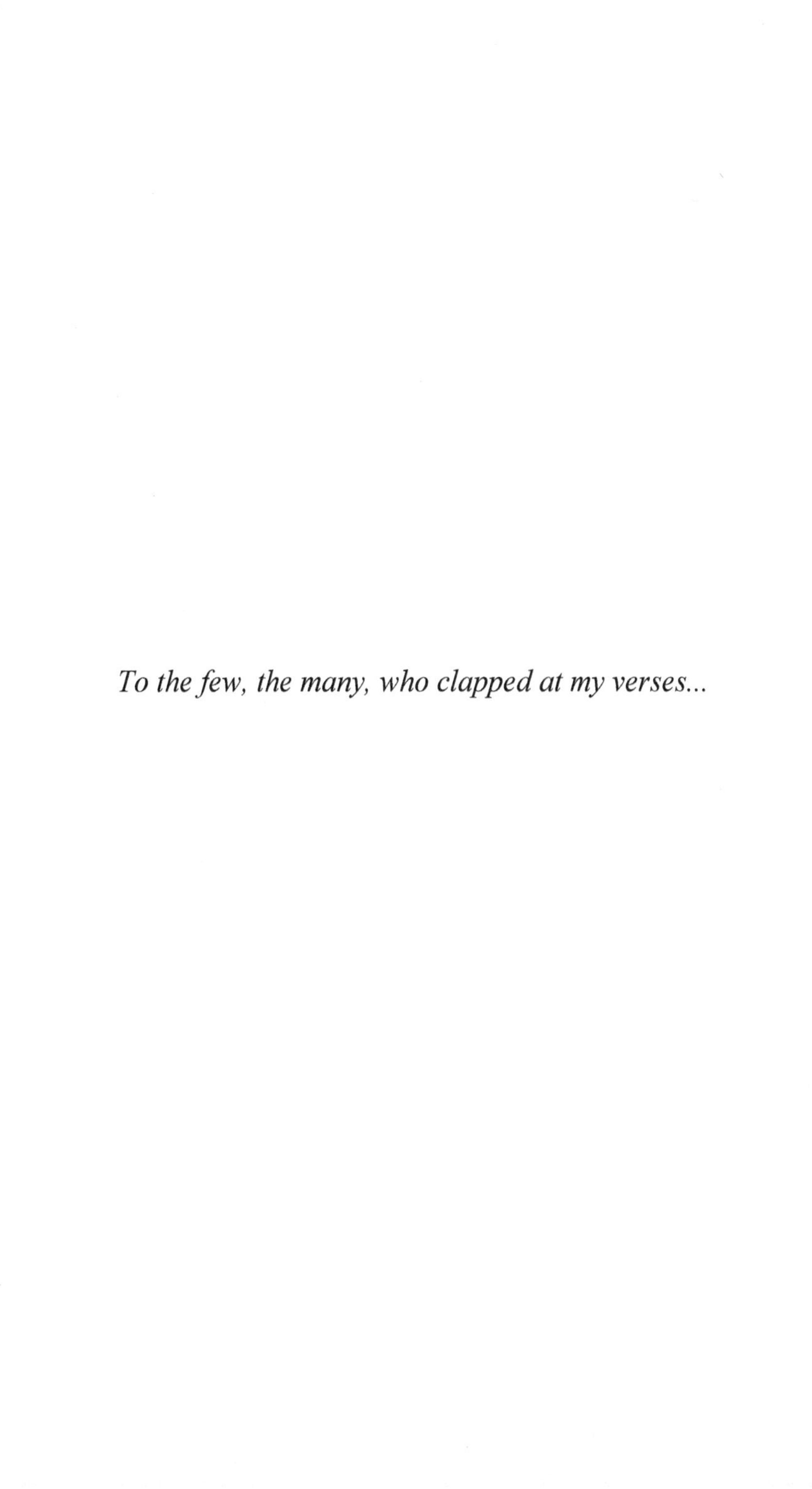

To the few, the many, who clapped at my verses...

CONTENTS

1. A Little Too Much

Once I met this distant
Relative on a bus.
It was the casual awkward avoidance
Accompanied by the 'No way
Not to notice' thing.
"Hey, I heard you were in the town."
I nodded in affirmation with
The best smile I could bring up.
"I heard you are only a visitor here now.
I heard you moved out in June.
Selfish people could care less
About one's whereabouts,
But how do you manage?"
As questions were rhetoric,
I was the listener.
"I heard you had meningitis last month.
Good that you have recovered.
I had heard from a friend
Of mine that his friend
Once had meningitis.
Poor lad thought it was
All better, only to find
Himself dead one morning.
I heard you got a promotion too.
You know, good news travels fast.
I heard you are going
Sydney next month.

Isn't it cold in there now?"
I had to get down at the next stop,
Without a word of courtesy
Would be unfair I thought.
"Oh dear! Don't you think
You hear a little too much."

2. Original Grief

Obliged to this night ride
Pouring out my agony
Aren't we the stardusts?
Who gave us emotions?
Why are these tiny atoms
Alive and feeling the whole lot
They could never afford?
Aren't we the stardusts?
All that wrap around me,
Mock at my mediocre matters.
The concealed face emoji tells
Almost the default state for long.
The nature, culture and future
Conspire against my wills.
The wind whistles to my wheezing,
The sun shuts down my eyes,
The rain might have been nice
But doesn't bother to approach
Unless I wear my white shoes.
Yet I pamper my brief case.
It isn't unprecedented,
Nor unanticipated.
But genuinely original grief
In my own manifestations.
Never have I ever thought
I would ever be alone in this ride.

3. Red

The sand, the sun and the waves
Seem similar yet disoriented each time.
That reddened sun looks so familiar;
As though the new born
Turning red with her first cry,
As though the face of a reluctant lad
Unwilling to go home as the sun sets,
As though the cheeks of a teenage girl
With butterflies and blushes,
As though the fury in a woman's eyes
Running her unsettling errands,
As though the red spots in a bed ridden granny's
Pale skin that marks her still alive.
How did I just picture a whole life
In the setting sun vanishing at the horizon?

4. Is This A Painting?

He looked at her
As though she was a painting.
He wondered at her brown eyes.
They shyly shifted their gaze.
He admired her blushed cheeks.
He dreamed over her curves.
He wished he could untie
Her beautiful imprisoned hair.
He longed for her trembling lips.
He gandered at her sensuous gasps.
He looked at her
As though she was a painting.

She was nervous standing alone,
Intolerable with his lustful gaze.
She felt uncomfortable
In her own body,
Threatened in her new dear dress,
Unsafe on her own land,
Unbearable with her raising heart,
Terrified with the histories.
She wasn't a painting.
She was a soul embodied.
Yet she couldn't stop him
As though she was a painting.

5. The Gardener

Your Highness! Accept these flowers
From your humble subject.
Those are the hand-picked cherry flowers.
The scent of it will take you to heavens.

Pleasure's mine to serve you
And this kingdom. I am the gardener.
Make me the king!
That should end all our agony.

Adore yourself with patience
And hear me before you command.
I am the gardener who knows
The bloodless battles you fought.

The rarest wild Taisies at
The garden's northest end
Have the juice that slowly poisons
One's head and one's senses.

When the generous king from Etheraile
Signed his land in your name.
Who do you think harvested
The whole lot of taisies in one eve?

The long-wired beans that grow
In summer shuts down one's liver.
With no symptoms for two happy days,
One's lively body faints to death.

When the reluctant king of Midwestland
Turned down your offer and was
Laid down in the coffin the second day.
Who do you think picked the ripened beans?

But the cherry flowers are soft and decent.
They give you their fantastic fragrance
And choke you to death giving you
A few moments to utter your last words.

So don't you think I know too much?
Make me the king and I shall
Give you a great funeral.
Drinking water will not save you.

That was the end of an era
For our kingdom and the land's histories.
With all due respect I take this Crown.
Indeed his highness deserves a great funeral.

6. To the Housefly I killed

Today I killed you.
And I add that in my portfolio.
For you aren't an easy target.
You're swift and dynamic.
And I am proud I killed you.
Why? You sat on my food.
Where else you had been?
In dirt and decayed?
You go on the ripe and the rotten,
On the food and the feces alike.
You may haven't suck my blood,
Nor you have bitten me hard.
But you spoiled my needs,
You soiled my dreams,
So I killed you.
You did hurt me.
You took away
What I needed the most
When I wanted it so badly.
So I killed you.
You aren't the romantic "fly"
As you had been for Blake.
You're the nuisance.
You and your tiny maggots
Are disgusting in my eyes.
So I killed you.
You ruptured my rapture.

You forcefully withdrew my plate.
You left my hedonic hunger unfed.
So I killed you
And you're the crime
I do not regret.

7. The Prospect of Love

Love doesn't but the prospect of love excites,
Like the sliding glance from eyes to lips excites,
Like the contagious laughter excites,
Like remembering the tiny details excites,
Like defending your silly argument excites,
Like searching for you in the crowd excites,
Like absurd abrupt conversation excites,
Like turning back after the goodbye excites,
Like planned coincidental meeting excites,
Like standing in silence in proximity excites,
Like declaring "I trust you" excites,
Like that crooked smile while they turn away excites,
Unlike the known- labelled -in contact love,
The prospect of love excites.

8. Stretch Marks

Pregnant with a zillion lives,
I've stretched my core to the skin
For you to thrive and flourish,
So to come out to see the light.
You sucked up all my strength.
All those sleepless nights, after
The sunny days, have worn me out.
This cracked crust bears witness
Of your birth and being.
You crawled on me.
You walked on me.
Yet you turned me dead brown.
I nurtured them
And I nurture you.
Yet you chop their heads.
Had you chosen to live
Together as kin and kith,
I would have harnessed
Many more stretch marks.

9. Undecipherable Melody

The unsettling waves in or around me
Plays an undecipherable melody.
On my watch, the highs and lows roar in the sea.
Yet somewhere something carves it into a beautiful
melody.

The lows touch the mourning pasts,
The highs deliberately those shadows cast.
Tricking the audience the magician casts
The masterpiece spell that forever would last.

The blacks and whites, the pure and tough
Gives a pattern, yet similar to a handcuff,
Blocks the throat with a roar said "enough"
That won't let out an unbearable cough.

For the keys are many, yet they are one,
For alone they don't but together, they're done
With the desires and duties of the possessed one.
I wish the locks, the blocks, the coughs and "enough"s
were undone.

10. Clear

Once it was all clear.
I stayed still and saw
Myself in that gathered drops.
The depth, the stones, the trench
Were all clear,
So were the sky, the clouds, the branches.
The tranquility of the moment
Was dear and clear.

But then came the rain.
The drops disturbed my peace.
"Which drop?" they asked.
No accusations shall revert.
Once it was all clear,
But now the depth is scary,
The sky falls down on me.
I could no longer see myself.

I stayed still and now
I am all wet and weary.
I could sense a frozen heart
"But it's just a breeze", they said.
Wet and weary and weak,
Even the breeze stormed at me.
Now drops are scarce
And the rain is ready to depart.

"What's wrong? The rain's gone."
They didn't know;
The branches still shed drops,
The depth's disturbed by dirt,
The tranquility is destroyed.
I stayed still and waited
For time may heal
And bring back my peace.

It's been a really long wait.
Time has settled everything down.
Yet it's still unclear.
The ripplings have gone
Sun has taken the last hanging drop.
"It's in your eyes", they said.
I am tired and teary.
Now the tears disturb my peace.

I couldn't stay still anymore.
I cried out my tears,
Not wholly for I had lost
The strength to go ahead.
Once it was all clear,
Not anymore now.
Let me dust it off and heal myself.
Once I will be clear again.

11. As Long As

In this water that life comes
Sustains and grows, yet perishes
If you are dipped in,
The worst when the earth
Beneath takes you in.
Behold the river, the streams
And flows, they capture
The grandeur and tricks you in.
When the feet sense
The touch, it's cool.
It's cooler to sink and float.
Yet you get the chills
Once it's up to your mouth.
Your throat's drowned,
You've voice no more.
Will that ferry fetch me?
No! I am just a picture
Of floating eyes and nose.
Here and there a fish bite,
Might have been ticklish
But not when you're breathless.
There from a long branch
A peacock stares at me.
I would have shared the same
If only a hope had been in me.
Shall these hands raise
To invite undesirable attention?

No! Powerless, strengthless,
Here I am at this horizon,
Scared to feel my last breath.
As long as the toe stands
I shall hold on.

12. A Physical Being

I exist in numbers; in years and days,
In volume and mass, in aadhaar too.
Prove my presence in the things I use,
The dress I wear, the books I own
And in the one I gave birth to too.
Count my needs in the food I eat,
In the bed I sleep, in the phone I hold.
Yes, I do exist as a physical being.

I am asked the howabouts of
My child, my parents, and even relatives
But never of this poor physical being.
Devoid of dreams and desires,
Be a puppet. Who the hell
Had taught me to dream?
To educate, to work and to make
The next move, I need consent.
And that is the biggest favour on earth.
Thank you honourable beings
For signing it. Am I owned?
Shall the words hurt me?
No! I am just a physical being.

I am like a virtual assistant.
Yell at me, shout at me,
I shall be always polite.
No other emojis to wear
Except the cute smileys.

Can I be angry at them?
Can I cry out loud before them?
No! I am just a physical being.

Inside something still whispers,
"Be free, write not what is dictated,
But what you feel, there you find
Your happiness." Alas! Who knows
This physical being has gave up
On happiness and desires only peace.
Shall these words heal me?
No! I was never wounded
'Cause I am just a physical being.

13. A Suicide Note

Let me die
To end this uneventful life,
Not to annoy anyone anymore,
To succeed in at least this attempt,
To off the burden of this poor earth.
Let me go
Away from my dears
With a note "I loved you".
Perhaps the lifeless corpse
Shall hear your praises and prayers
That I had longed for.
Let me cut this vein
To slowly drain this life.
I shall not if only I could hear
"I am here for you".
No! I can't hear that.
Let me take this pain
To end all my pains.

14. Chaining Assets

Free are the birds with no boundaries.
Chained are the ones who built a nest
For they return from time to time
And that limits their radius.
Wings alone won't let you fly.

15. The Refrigerated Fight

We sat across the dining table,
Face to face, yet saw the faces
Of people miles away on our screens.
There was a fight, fresh and bleeding,
I was hurt. And I tried exposing my wound.
He was obsessed with his pain.
So was I?
Couldn't throw out this fight,
It's still fresh and bleeding.
Let me refrigerate it for now.
Hours passed, so did days.
It's now frozen and tasteless.
It's time to throw away this.
I put on a smile and looked at the mirror.
I still saw the tears in my eyes.

16. When Sorrow Strikes

When the thorns of sorrow strike,
The eyes go blind so do all the senses
And gloom and numbness take
Over the kingdom and mark the fences.

"Let alone sorrow enter the gates",
A command so rude travels the kingdom.
As though heavy are the dates,
Time now treads lightly and numb.

"Let peace be seen from afar and across
The gates that there must await",
The poor soul pleas and makes her vows
"I shall find ways to open the gate".

All that I sense is unfair sorrow.
Before my eyes and beyond my reign,
Grief and grey all the news follow
Yet a hope arises midst the pain
For "Surely, with hardship comes ease",
Said the One who promised peace.

17. Theft in the Neighbourhood

"Ah Ronnie! Days just pass by.
Nothing serious or curious happens around.
Oh you heard it too?
Yes, there was a theft in the neighborhood.
But never mind, it's not our home.
Some strangers entered the house by force.
'Mr. Mike was shot,
His daughter raped
And his wife injured',
They say.
But never mind, it's not our home.
Remember Brownie? Their dog!
Luckily it was only tranquilized.
Poor lad! I have taken him home.
Isn't it inhumane to orphan a pet?
The house and appliances are badly damaged.
It was an unfortunate incident.
But never mind, it's not our home.
I was watching Netflix
When I heard the commotion.
For a moment I thought
My earphones were damaged.
You see these are the new ones
You sent from London last week.
Lucky! They are fine.
We got the news from the newspaper boy.
No! I don't know if valuables are lost.

You see, I don't peep into others' matters.
However their car seems missing.
But never mind, it's not our home.
'There was a similar incident
In the house before it in the lane',
They say.
They have alarmed our mom
Hinting the next is ours.
But you don't worry.
I don't let any trouble seeking habits in this house.
Sarah! See who is at the door.
SARAHH!
Rr...Ron...Ronnie, I think they are home."
Reader, never mind, it's not our home.

18. Hibernation

Helpless am I
As though I fall off a cliff.
My arms reach no clutches,
My feet feel no touches,
My head gives no solutions,
My mind has no emotions,
And I am free.
Now needs no worry.

A while ago,
My feelings were shattered,
My heart unsecured,
My arms were burdened,
My feet were detained,
And I was in captivity
And my worries infinity.

Now as helpless as I lay,
I take this moment to hibernate;
My arms are now loosened,
My feet now unrestrained,
My head safe and sound,
My mind now unbound
And I am free.
Now needs no worry.

Let thus fall,
Scatter my hassle,
Clean up this muddle,
Conserve my power
To bring back the vigour,
To live the ardour,
To bounce back harder,
And be the me;
The all that I can be.
Yes, at the end of this fall
I shall wake to a life afresh.

19. Forever Unknown!

"Hey Ram Hey Ram"
Shot dead the one who had an abode
For Ram in his own heart.
But Ram had changed so much with Gandhi's death.
They say he prefers temple more than hearts.
So they have made the best plain
Over the corpses and tears and blood
They are used to cries of pain
But who they are, are forever unknown.

They thought India a land with borders
But forgot it's a nation in our blood.
They thought we might kill our brothers
But we have pledged "all Indians are my brothers".
They throw bones to tempt us
But we are not dogs they must know.
Oh India! Beware of them
For who they are, are forever unknown.
They make life at the cost of this nation
But we must stand to defend our mother
To uphold her colours
To polish her assets
To accept her varieties
And live with "unity in diversity"
For they want us to forget;
We are Gandhi
We are Buddha

We are Abdul Kalam
Oh India! Beware of them
For who they are, are forever unknown.

They will never have the crisis we anticipate
For they are ready to sell us.
We must know where we stand
For we may lose this land,
Can't complain
Can't protest
Can't trust our own senses
For who they are, are forever unknown.
Oh India! Beware of them.
Raise your voice now or never.

20. The Frozen Heart

Devoid of feelings the heart wept
An undecipherable melody of its kind
That none had heard or known before
Yet a solace to the soul the tears trenched!

One lash aches, but a thousand freeze.
The evolved soul thus denies not
The truth for silly self-exile.
It bears the mark of pain and defence.

It begins with a pain, follows a numbness,
Then slowly let the heart be frozen;
Quite aware of the dreadful stillness
Though no more a name is chosen.

Hold! Hold! Let the Reason speak,
"If it's for Him, He shall defend."

21. Cries

Landed on earth with the loudest cry,
Then it turned to the single language
For milk, for sleep, for everything else
All I did was cry aloud.
And then I learnt the crooked world
And as selfish I grew the best way found
To achieve my goal was cry better.
And then I cried when sent to school
And then again when I left my school.
Then I cried at mother's warnings
Of a world that seemed more terrible than forests
Though all was true I later realised.
Then I cried when I left my home
To another home by social norm.
And then I cried when his voice rose;
A cry as useless as a white pencil.
Then I cried for another life
To land on earth to repeat the lines.
Then I cried when their voices rose.
(My mother too would have cried;
Then I never thought)
Then when I had grown enough
Ego to withhold my precious tears,
The heart couldn't stand and did burst.
In that painful cry I breathed my last.
Now cries have begun
But I hear no more.

22. Woven Spider Web

My heart's a woven spider web
Made with tender delicate feelings.
Caught was in it a tiny-spider-thought
And found an ancient sense of belongingness.

It grew on its own enormous power
Still tender was the base.

As heavy as a cloud,
It hovered and moved at times.

Little did the heart notice
That it had grown bigger;
Helpless but the pen helped.

Still tender is my heart.

23. The Midnight Frost

The midnight frost is forever still
Till the morn breaks up the hill
Without a breath's tender touch
Without a foot's clustered clutch
As if for the silence a chilling couch.

The midnight frost is quite inert
As if she were a hurtless introvert
Submitted to one's self in devotion
Yet reflects the whole in some strange fashion
And a great witness with no hesitation.

The midnight frost is forever still
Till the morn breaks up the hill.
Alive was she in the deepest silence.
None noticed, none did defence.
None will miss her in her absence.

24. Devil's Silence

Before me lays a glass.
It's so huge, a sphere encircling me.
There's a fading paint
That fades each day;
More and more day by day.

Now that I can see through
A bright brutal massacre,
I wonder why do they kill?
What do they fear?
What wrong have they done?

Though no sound is heard
The glass saves me from the cries
And I am in a devil like silence
Watching like a stone
Dead bodies falling in each blink.

They say they are terrorists
But they are terror stricken.
Had they called the God another name
They wouldn't have suffered so much.
Their mistake was their faith.

The scene moves closer each day
And one day they will break this glass as well
And then I shall scream to death
And break this devil's silence
For I too had believed.

25. The Refugee Camp

Had he but spared the forbidden fruit
Heaven shall have witnessed more crimes.
But a whole new race was brought
On here on earth as refugees.

"Oh men! Live, love, eat and drink
But do not exceed." God said the farewell note.
Oh the Mercy chose to save the disobedient man.
And here on earth we are refugees.

None but the most Merciful could grant
Such a lovely grand refugee camp.
Here we lived, ruled and conquered
But forgot 'we are refugees.'

Erase the green, pollute the blue
And remove the strong dark mountains.
Worship the sun, worship the moon
And worship all that u may find.

Create myths, write legends
And perish in fantasies.
Choose the best fool to rule
And protest on the land's laws.

Use, misuse and then abuse.
Exploit, humiliate and then repeat.
Destroy the tiny globe in the vast universe.
But do not ask for another refugee camp.

26. The sparrow drove the Pegasus

The sparrow drove the Pegasus.
Why if she could fly alone?

For she owned a heart that throbs
To quench the parches of those nerves.

That bleeds her throat in thirst
Never allows her to sing at ease.

The bloody and bloodless bonds
Knocked down her little wings.

The sparrow drove the Pegasus
To go beyond her reach.

27. Let the pillow alone know her name

Veiled in rage she came out.
Ah! The light she had seen at last.
She had stood at door with doubt.
Alas, now came out with a blast.

She had deep stories to tell
But chose to shout the least of words.
Fearful if those drops may fell,
She herself adorned against all worlds.

Too proud to think she's weak,
That all may think but she's not.
She is strong; strong at the peak
And trench of the heart's every note.

And then she knew the eyes would fail.
So she did come with her veil
To hide and cover all her shame;
Let the pillow alone know her name.

28. Alice is on the deck

None on either side to beck.
The sea rages as wild as when
Eloped the daughter of Lord Ullin.
She lost her love to this rage,
Who loved her deep at the stage,
Who with love, kissed her tears
And held her hand against all fears.
She now stands sunk in sorrow,
Lost her hopes for the morrow.
The dear departed lies here,
Fallen cold and dead so near.
"Let you rage upon me too.
Spare me not. You may do."
Shouted she at the tides
Or the spirits at heaven hides.
The ship went still all at once.
The waves got calm with no bounce.
"Hey! You can't win me O' waves,
I must jump into your caves.
My love's gone, my life's gone.
All lost, I stand here alone."
To give her thoughts a great pause,
From the clouds came an albatross.
"Alice, think again and jump not.
All they needed waves have got."
"O big bird! Who are you?"
Why warn me not to do?"

"From the heavens I come, an albatross"
"Sent by my love I do guess"
"No, but by the ancient mariner,
My ever regretting betrayed killer
To warn you not to slain
An innocent life in vain,
To let you know your whole
Life you regret killing a pure soul."
"I kill myself for I am alone
I live no more to regret upon"
"Soul never reaches heaven
Until called upon by fate.
Love's life but life isn't all in
Love; stay back it's better late."
Said so flew the albatross.
Stepped back to life Alice.

29. Ode to a Dragon Fly

Who named thou the dragon fly
Unseen have they thy colourless wings?
Thy swift moves in the nearer sky,
Rain or summer, thou here brings?

Some foolish folk called thee thy name.
Who else should a poor creature
Name a name that spits flame?
Thou are a tiny beauty of a big nature.

Alas! In a world so wild and crazy
Where men kill men for non-sense,
Who seeks a fair justice for thee?
Here thou have no foes and friends.

Seek thy justice in the hereafter
For here thy pain causes mere laughter.

30. The Death of a Foster Child

I bid thee farewell my child.
Let's depart in tear
Than be together in fear.
Thou lost thy life alive.
Now no apologies, no hopes.
I kept you long
And you made me strong.
Now leave these weak arms
And seek thy fortune.
I bury thee with pain
Than hug you in vain,
Though I know
In the dark deep Talent grows not.
This is no death to you
But a way to rebirth.
May you be born again
In a safe and bold hand
That fears not the loss
And submits not to fate.
May you never hate
Me nor may God curse me.
I bid thee farewell
Good bye. Good bye. Good bye.

31. Grace in Scare

Withdrawn by fear, fail not to witness
The beauty baffling before thy eye
For then that's alike a treasure beneath thy
Feet that thou never did even guess.

Someone trembles- the heartbeat fastens
On the very sight of the lightning.
Do those silver sparks seem so frightening?
Sharpens the clouds' whisper or hardens?

Yonder someone shuts the eyes in fear,
Upon a height some call scary.
When all that climb has made him weary,
Isn't it a beautiful sight, far but near?

It's funny when someone fears; even
Amidst of a crowd, or when she
Spots a spider or snake and the most funny
Fear of all to fly in an aeroplane.

Call it a joke or not. It isn't.
For all fears open a way to death.
But why fear to welcome the last breath?
For it may enter with or with no hint.

Life is alive when you do fight
And fail not enjoy by fear withdrawn.
All I fear is the darkness alone
And the One who owns all the light.

32. Taming the Time

Taming the time is an art
Unknown to all ever born
But he who has the cart
And learnt what he had owned.
His heart beats with the rhythm of
The feet that carry him off.
He knows Time trots, caters and gallops.
Yet he carries the bundle of hopes.
He has known the art of balancing
And rides evenly days and nights.
Behold him and the Time is dancing
To his desires and his rights.
When Time reaches the stable of death,
You would know he has lived all his breath.

33. Nature's Prisoner

Yonder the flowers fell in silence.
Gone are their gifted fragrance.
Sorrow shall not bring thy tears
For truly they were never yours.
Though thou did behold their charm,
At distance they did no good no harm;
Unknown of this silent admirer
They pretended nothing but what they were.
And here's the wind hold dead leaves
So lightly with no sighs no heaves;
Singing in ears undecipherable melody.
Take me too in your journey.
And the sky is prettier at the night
With the lovely moon smiling bright.
When all asleep in this silence,
Oh Night! Why your beauty is so intense?
Truly, my heart you did conquer
And my eyes you did capture
And left me stand as an admirer.
Oh nature! I am your prisoner.
But I love these chains and this trap
For I have fallen on your lap.
I would have written even more
If I were born even before.
Helpless to know what years would leave,
Let me write when you are still alive.

34. Paradoxes

When a single star makes the whole day bright,
With a million stars it's still dark is the night.
When tears stand synonymous with pain,
All we try is to smile in vain.
When hope is lost and heart is broken,
It's still "I'm fine" the words are spoken.
On the whole, this life is nothing but a big lie,
Or a pretended truth that we adore with no shy.
Call me rude for with you this I share
For all these paradoxes I no longer care.

35. Ode to Death

None in the world has a promised tomorrow
And you do come with o days to borrow.
No suns no moons can ever hold you still
And for no moment no second delay you will.
If you are too certain to ignore you,
Then why should I ever fear you?
None shook your hand ever returned.
It seems you're fairer than cruel we pretend.
If you're so fair never return to,
Then why should I ever fear you?
I feel your shadow hovering around
With silence and darkness in the background
For that's the picture the world gave me
And it may be true or may not be.
What if you're gentle! I used to think,
And let my soul depart in a blink.
Then that would be a fair farewell
And a warm welcome to the eternal;
The world of justice I would behold
And give my diary the last fold.
So come for me when I can say:
I have no regrets if I now pass away.
If I had done all I should do,
Then why should I ever fear you?
Be brave and you may conquer me
When I can still stand and see
And let me not remain a mere mass

And wait for your arrival to pass.
So come to me when least expected
And take me all at once.

36. Tonight I read my Father's Diary

Tonight I read my father's diary.
Pages smelled of sweat and were weary.
The font was ugly but words- simple
And told a story of tears on his dimple.
A rueful smile had often brightened his face.
His longings were all to give us an embrace.
But often failed and hugged us with prayers.
These words are alone for many years.

We have lived in his light
That he had given burning bright,
Melting and dying day by day
And all unknown we do here play.
Watching those drops of wax falling,
I see tears, from his eyes, dropping
Like a pearl rolling down those cheeks
That, only our smiles, sincerely seeks.

O' father! Let me kiss those dimples now
Though wet with tears by now
To thank you for burning all your youth
But – I can't do enough – to tell the truth.

37. The Smiling Moon

Yonder the moon smiles bright tonight,
A smile brighter and wider than last night.
It seems the stars have withdrawn their light.
Trust me; you have conquered my sight,
And I walk to you in this twilight.

This night owns a silence and a deep quietness.
No snores, no slams shall disturb its darkness
And in my sight it's only your brightness.
I'm walking to you to erase your loneliness
To smile bright but with yours a little less.

None knows that I come to you
And I know not why I this do,
Though I know my feet can't take to you.
For a reason unknown I'm walking to you.
But you're too lovely to go back to.

I see not the thorns nor pits so deep
But your smile that does my path keep.
At you, anyone shall forget to weep
Though he holds tears to a high heap.
You're so lovely that I despise my sleep.

I can hear the whistling wind whispering
Not to me but to the clouds above hovering
To hide you to prevent me from seeing
You so bright in this vast dark high sky shining.

Yet senselessly to you I'm walking.

I had walked long it appear
That my house is shorter than a dot from here.
Did I alone come so far without fear?
No! You dragged me, now tell me dear,
Why you are even now not near?

Don't tell me you were deceiving me
And all this time you were laughing at me,
Like any other pleasure in this world I see
You too swallowed my time unnecessarily.
Your smile is cruel now I see.

When dawn breaks in you'll leave me alone.
The sky will have the sun to adorn.
Into the silence, now enters a fearful tone.
I shouldn't have, for no reason, so far gone.
My tired legs, now, won't take me home.

38. The Seeker of Sorrow

Man is the seeker of sorrow.
Willingly or not he is,
For he does often borrow
Tears to erase his ease.

Though he likes not he does
Remain in immemorial grief.
Though he longs not he does
Think things go wrong what if!

It seems sorrow, for men, is default
And happiness comes in like a guest
And it leaves soon or may halt
For a moment or two, quenches not quest.

The seeker of sorrow when this read
May now argue or nod his head.

39. The Story of a Fool

I'll tell you the story of a fool.
He was given the very sharp tool
And was asked to carve a statue
Of his own choice and his own view.
So as to stand as an imprint of his life
That would survive even after his life.

He thought and thought on what to make.
His doubts gave him a big headache.
To all he met, he asked and asked.
All, before him, preferred to be masked.
He spent his life dipped in thoughts
But couldn't choose one and make it the best.
He passed away with the same thoughts
Leaving the tool whose sharpness he never did test!

40. Silences

Sometimes silence means peace;
Peace- a divine effect of battle.
Sometimes silence means to cease.
Cease the life; how fatal?
Sometimes silence means alone,
Alone counting each moment.
Sometimes silence means to adorn,
Adorn with no sign no comment.
Sometimes silence makes you terrible,
Terrible with the pain of loneliness.
Sometimes silence makes you capable,
Capable to face any hardness.
What may! Silence is all around,
That on me and you surround.

ABOUT THE AUTHOR

Rashida M. C. prefers to be unseen, unknown, unlamented, and undecipherable. Yet, she hopes to be read, re-read, and deciphered through these lines.

Have you written a book?
Publish it for free today!

Writer's Pocket is a publication house based in Vadodara, Gujarat. Established in 2016, we have a community of over 50,000 writers whose works we have published.

To publish your book with us for free, scan this QR code:

You can also reach out to us at:

Phone number: (+91) 8200 377 328
Email address: editor@writerspocket.com

www.ingramcontent.com/pod-product-compliance
Lightning Source LLC
LaVergne TN
LVHW091219180726
843490LV00007B/2845